The Rise Of The Dutch Republic

Volume 12

by

John Lothrop Motley

Double9 BOOKS

The Rise Of The Dutch Republic
Volume 12
by John Lothrop Motley

ISBN: 978-93-75552-25-3

Published by

DOUBLE 9 BOOKS
2/13-B, Ansari Road
Daryaganj, New Delhi – 110002
info@double9books.com
www.double9books.com
Tel. 011-40042856

ABOUT THE AUTHOR

John Lothrop Motley was an American historian and diplomat renowned for his detailed studies on the political and social evolution of the Netherlands. Born in Dorchester, Massachusetts, to Thomas Motley and Ann Lothrop Motley, he developed a deep interest in European history and diplomacy that would define his intellectual pursuits. Educated at prestigious institutions, he later embarked on a career that combined scholarship and public service, producing some of the most significant historical works of his time. His best-known writings include The Rise of the Dutch Republic and The History of the United Netherlands, which vividly depict the Netherlands' struggle for independence and political identity. Motley's historical approach blended meticulous research with a literary narrative style that captured the moral and emotional dimensions of history. Alongside his literary achievements, he served as a diplomat, representing the United States abroad with distinction. His legacy endures as that of a historian who united rigorous scholarship with eloquent expression and human insight.

CONTENTS

1567 [CHAPTER IX., PART 2]

It was then that Noircarmes and his "seven sleepers" showed that they were awake. Early in January, 1567, that fierce soldier, among whose vices slothfulness was certainly never reckoned before or afterwards, fell upon the locksmith's army at Zannoy, while the Seigneur de Rassinghem attacked the force at Waterlots on the same day. Noircarmes destroyed half his enemies at the very first charge. The ill-assorted rabble fell asunder at once. The preacher fought well, but his undisciplined force fled at the first sight of the enemy. Those who carried arquebusses threw them down without a single discharge, that they might run the faster. At least a thousand were soon stretched dead upon the field; others were hunted into the river. Twenty-six hundred, according to the Catholic accounts, were exterminated in an hour.

Rassinghem, on his part, with five or six hundred regulars, attacked Teriel's force, numbering at least twice as many. Half of these were soon cut to pieces and put to flight. Six hundred, however, who had seen some service, took refuge in the cemetery of Waterlots. Here, from behind the stone wall of the inclosure, they sustained the attack of the Catholics with some spirit. The repose of the dead in the quiet country church-yard was disturbed by the uproar of a most sanguinary conflict. The temporary fort was soon carried, and the Huguenots retreated into the church. A rattling arquebusade was poured in upon them as they struggled in the narrow doorway. At least four hundred corpses were soon strewn among the ancient graves. The rest were hunted, into the church, and from the church into the belfry. A fire was then made in the steeple and kept up till all were roasted or suffocated. Not a man escaped.

This was the issue in the first stricken field in the Netherlands, for the cause of religious liberty. It must be confessed that it was not very encouraging to the lovers of freedom. The partisans of government were elated, in proportion to the apprehension which had been felt for the result of this rising in the Walloon country. "These good hypocrites," wrote a correspondent of Orange, "are lifting up their heads like so many dromedaries. They are becoming unmanageable with pride." The Duke of Aerschot and Count Meghem gave great banquets in Brussels, where all the good chevaliers drank deep in honor of the victory, and to the health of his

Majesty and Madame. "I saw Berlaymont just go by the window," wrote Schwartz to the Prince. "He was coming from Aerschot's dinner with a face as red as the Cardinal's new hat."

On the other hand, the citizens of Valenciennes were depressed in equal measure with the exultation of their antagonists. There was no more talk of seven sleepers now, no more lunettes stuck upon lances, to spy the coming forces of the enemy. It was felt that the government was wide awake, and that the city would soon see the impending horrors without telescopes. The siege was pressed more closely. Noircarmes took up a commanding position at Saint Armand, by which he was enabled to cut off all communication between the city and the surrounding country. All the villages in the neighborhood were pillaged; all the fields laid waste. All the infamies which an insolent soldiery can inflict upon helpless peasantry were daily enacted. Men and women who attempted any communication—with the city, were murdered in cold blood by hundreds. The villagers were plundered of their miserable possessions, children were stripped naked in the midst of winter for the sake of the rags which covered them; matrons and virgins were sold at public auction by the tap of drum; sick and wounded wretches were burned over slow fires, to afford amusement to the soldiers. In brief, the whole unmitigated curse which military power inflamed by religious bigotry can embody, had descended upon the heads of these unfortunate provincials who had dared to worship God in Christian churches without a Roman ritual.

Meantime the city maintained, a stout heart still. The whole population were arranged under different banners. The rich and poor alike took arms to defend the walls which sheltered them. The town paupers were enrolled in three companies, which bore the significant title of the "Tons-nulls" or the "Stark-nakeds," and many was the fierce conflict delivered outside the gates by men, who, in the words of a Catholic then in the city, might rather be taken for "experienced veterans than for burghers and artisans." At the same time, to the honor of Valenciennes, it must be stated, upon the same incontestable authority, that not a Catholic in the city was injured or insulted. The priests who had remained there were not allowed to say mass, but they never met with an opprobrious word or look from the people.

The inhabitants of the city called upon the confederates for assistance. They also issued an address to the Knights of the Fleece; a paper which narrated the story of their wrongs in pathetic and startling language. They appealed to those puissant and illustrious chevaliers to prevent the perpetration of the great wrong which was now impending over so many innocent heads. "Wait not," they said, "till the thunderbolt has fallen, till the deluge has overwhelmed us, till the fires already blazing have laid the land in coals and ashes, till no other course be possible, but to abandon the country in its desolation to foreign barbarity. Let the cause of the oppressed come to your ears. So shall your conscience become a shield of iron; so shall the happiness of a whole country witness before the angels, of your truth to his Majesty, in the cause of his true grandeur and glory."

These stirring appeals to an order of which Philip was chief, Viglius chancellor, Egmont, Mansfeld, Aerschot, Berlaymont, and others, chevaliers, were not likely to produce much effect. The city could rely upon no assistance in those high quarters.

Meantime, however, the bold Brederode was attempting a very extensive diversion, which, if successful, would have saved Valenciennes and the whole country beside. That eccentric personage, during the autumn and winter had been creating disturbances in various parts of the country. Wherever he happened to be established, there came from the windows of his apartments a sound of revelry and uproar. Suspicious characters in various costumes thronged his door and dogged his footsteps. At the same time the authorities felt themselves obliged to treat him with respect. At Horn he had entertained many of the leading citizens at a great banquet.—The-health-of-the-beggars had been drunk in mighty potations, and their shibboleth had resounded through the house. In the midst of the festivities, Brederode had suspended a beggar's-medal around the neck of the burgomaster, who had consented to be his guest upon that occasion, but who had no intention of enrolling himself in the fraternities of actual or political mendicants. The excellent magistrate, however, was near becoming a member of both. The emblem by which he had been conspicuously adorned proved very embarrassing to him upon his recovery from the effects of his orgies with the "great beggar," and he was subsequently punished for his imprudence by the confiscation of half his property.

Early in January, Brederode had stationed himself in his city of Viane. There, in virtue of his seignorial rights, he had removed all statues and other popish emblems from the churches, performing the operation, however, with much quietness and decorum. He had also collected many disorderly men at arms in this city, and had strengthened its fortifications, to resist, as he said, the threatened attacks of Duke Eric of Brunswick and his German mercenaries. A printing-press was established in the place, whence satirical pamphlets, hymn-books, and other pestiferous productions, were constantly issuing to the annoyance of government. Many lawless and uproarious individuals enjoyed the Count's hospitality. All the dregs and filth of the provinces, according to Doctor Viglius, were accumulated at Viane as in a cesspool. Along the placid banks of the Lech, on which river the city stands, the "hydra of rebellion" lay ever coiled and threatening.

Brederode was supposed to be revolving vast schemes, both political and military, and Margaret of Parma was kept in continual apprehension by the bravado of this very noisy conspirator. She called upon William of Orange, as usual, for assistance. The Prince, however, was very ill- disposed to come to her relief. An extreme disgust for the policy of the government already began to, characterize his public language. In the autumn and winter he had done all that man could do for the safety of the monarch's crown, and for the people's happiness. His services in Antwerp have been recorded. As soon as he could tear himself from that city, where the magistrates and all classes of citizens clung to him as to their only saviour, he had hastened to tranquillize the provinces of Holland, Zeland, and Utrecht. He had made arrangements in the principal cities there upon the same basis which he had adopted in Antwerp, and to which Margaret had consented in August. It was quite out of the question to establish order without permitting the reformers, who constituted much the larger portion of the population, to have liberty of religious exercises at some places, not consecrated, within the cities.

At Amsterdam, for instance, as he informed the Duchess, there were swarms of unlearned, barbarous people, mariners and the like, who could by no means perceive the propriety of doing their preaching in the open country, seeing that the open country, at that season, was quite under water.—Margaret's gracious suggestion that, perhaps, something might be done with boats, was also considered inadmissible. "I know not," said Orange, "who could have advised your highness to make such a proposition." He informed her, likewise; that the barbarous mariners had a clear right to their preaching; for the custom had already been established previously to the August treaty, at a place called the "Lastadge," among the wharves. "In the name of God, then," wrote Margaret; "let them continue to preach in the Lastadge." This being all the barbarians wanted, an Accord, with the full consent of the Regent, was drawn up at Amsterdam and the other northern cities. The Catholics kept churches and cathedrals, but in the winter season, the greater part of the population obtained permission to worship God upon dry land, in warehouses and dock-yards.

Within a very few weeks, however, the whole arrangement was coolly cancelled by the Duchess, her permission revoked, and peremptory prohibition of all preaching within or without the walls proclaimed. The government was growing stronger. Had not Noircarmes and Rassinghem cut to pieces three or four thousand of these sectaries marching to battle under parsons, locksmiths, and similar chieftains? Were not all lovers of good government "erecting their heads like dromedaries?"

It may easily be comprehended that the Prince could not with complacency permit himself to be thus perpetually stultified by a weak, false, and imperious woman. She had repeatedly called upon him when she was appalled at the tempest and sinking in the ocean; and she had as constantly disavowed his deeds and reviled his character when she felt herself in safety again. He had tranquillized the old Batavian provinces, where the old Batavian spirit still lingered, by his personal influence and his unwearied exertions. Men of all ranks and religions were grateful for his labors. The Reformers had not gained much, but they were satisfied. The Catholics retained their churches, their property, their consideration. The states of Holland had voted him fifty thousand florins, as an acknowledgment of his efforts in restoring peace. He had refused the present. He was in debt, pressed for money, but he did not choose, as he informed Philip, "that men should think his actions governed by motives of avarice or particular interest, instead of the true affection which he bore to his Majesty's service and the good of the country." Nevertheless, his back was hardly turned before all his work was undone by the Regent.

A new and important step on the part of the government had now placed him in an attitude of almost avowed rebellion. All functionaries, from governors of provinces down to subalterns in the army, were required to take a new oath of allegiance, "novum et hactenua inusitatum religionia juramentum," as the Prince characterized it, which was, he said, quite equal to the inquisition. Every man who bore his Majesty's commission was ordered solemnly to pledge himself to obey the orders of government, every where, and against every person, without limitation or restriction.—Count Mansfeld, now "factotum at Brussels," had taken the oath with great fervor. So had Aerachot, Berlaymont, Meghem, and, after a little wavering, Egmont. Orange spurned the proposition. He had taken oaths enough which he had never broken, nor intended now to break: He was ready still to do every thing conducive to the real interest of the monarch. Who dared do more was no true servant to the government, no true lover of the country. He would never disgrace himself by a blind pledge, through which he might be constrained to do acts detrimental, in his opinion, to the safety of the crown, the happiness of the commonwealth, and his own honor. The alternative presented he willingly embraced. He renounced all his offices, and desired no longer to serve a government whose policy he did not approve, a King by whom he was suspected.

His resignation was not accepted by the Duchess, who still made efforts to retain the services of a man who was necessary to her administration. She begged him, notwithstanding the purely defensive and watchful attitude which he had now assumed, to take measures that Brederode should abandon his mischievous courses. She also reproached the Prince with having furnished that personage with artillery for his fortifications. Orange answered, somewhat contemptuously, that he was not Brederode's keeper, and had no occasion to meddle with his affairs. He had given him three small field-pieces, promised long ago; not that he mentioned that circumstance as an excuse for the donation. "Thank God," said he, "we have always had the liberty in this country of making to friends or relatives what presents we liked, and methinks that things have come to a pretty pass when such trifles are scrutinized." Certainly, as Suzerain of Viane, and threatened with invasion in his seignorial rights, the Count might think himself justified in strengthening the bulwarks of his little stronghold, and the Prince could hardly be deemed very seriously to endanger the safety of the crown by the insignificant present which had annoyed the Regent.

It is not so agreeable to contemplate the apparent intimacy which the Prince accorded to so disreputable a character, but Orange was now in hostility to the government, was convinced by evidence, whose accuracy time was most signally to establish, that his own head, as well as many others, were already doomed to the block, while the whole country was devoted to abject servitude, and he was therefore disposed to look with more indulgence upon the follies of those who were endeavoring, however weakly and insanely, to avert the horrors which he foresaw. The time for reasoning had passed. All that true wisdom and practical statesmanship could suggest, he had already placed at the disposal of a woman who stabbed him in the back even while she leaned upon his arm—of a king who had already drawn his death warrant, while reproaching his "cousin of Orange" for want of confidence in the royal friendship. Was he now to attempt the subjugation of his country by interfering with the proceedings of men whom he had no power to command, and who, at least, were attempting to oppose tyranny? Even if he should do so, he was perfectly aware of the reward, reserved for his loyalty. He liked not such honors as he foresaw for all those who had ever interposed between the monarch and his vengeance. For himself he had the liberation of a country, the foundation of a free commonwealth to achieve. There was much work for those hands before he should fall a victim to the crowned assassin.

Early in February, Brederode, Hoogstraaten, Horn, and some other gentlemen, visited the Prince at Breda. Here it is supposed the advice of Orange was asked concerning the new movement contemplated by Brederode. He was bent upon presenting a new petition to the Duchess with great solemnity. There is no evidence to show that the Prince approved the step, which must have seemed to him superfluous, if not puerile. He probably regarded the matter with indifference. Brederode, however, who was fond of making demonstrations, and thought himself endowed with a genius for such work, wrote to the Regent for letters of safe conduct that he might come to Brussels with his petition. The passports were contemptuously refused. He then came to Antwerp, from which city he forwarded the document to Brussels in a letter.

By this new Request, the exercise of the reformed religion was claimed as a right, while the Duchess was summoned to disband the forces which she had been collecting, and to maintain in good faith the "August" treaty. These claims were somewhat bolder than those of the previous April, although the liberal party was much weaker and the confederacy entirely disbanded. Brederode, no doubt, thought it good generalship to throw the last loaf of bread into the enemy's camp before the city should surrender. His haughty tone was at once taken down by Margaret of Parma. "She wondered," she said, "what manner of nobles these were, who, after requesting, a year before, to be saved only from the inquisition, now presumed to talk about preaching in the cities." The concessions of August had always been odious, and were now canceled. "As for you and your accomplices," she continued to the Count, "you will do well to go to your homes at once without meddling with public affairs, for, in case of disobedience, I shall deal with you as I shall deem expedient."

Brederode not easily abashed, disregarded the advice, and continued in Antwerp. Here, accepting the answer of the Regent as a formal declaration of hostilities, he busied himself in levying troops in and about the city.

Orange had returned to Antwerp early in February. During his absence, Hoogstraaten had acted as governor at the instance of the Prince and of the Regent. During the winter that nobleman, who was very young and very fiery, had carried matters with a high hand, whenever there had been the least attempt at sedition. Liberal in principles, and the devoted friend of Orange, he was disposed however to prove that the champions of religious liberty were not the patrons of sedition. A riot occurring in the cathedral, where a violent mob were engaged in defacing whatever was left to deface in that church, and in heaping insults on the papists at their worship, the little Count, who, says a Catholic contemporary, "had the courage of a lion," dashed in among them, sword in hand, killed three upon the spot, and, aided by his followers, succeeded in slaying, wounding, or capturing all the rest. He had also tracked the ringleader of the tumult to his lodging, where he had caused him to be arrested at midnight, and hanged at once in his shirt without any form of trial. Such rapid proceedings little resembled the calm and judicious moderation of Orange upon all occasions, but they certainly might have sufficed to convince Philip that all antagonists of the inquisition were not heretics and outlaws. Upon the arrival of the Prince in Antwerp, it was considered advisable that Hoogstraaten should remain associated with him in the temporary government of the city.

During the month of February, Brederode remained in Antwerp, secretly enrolling troops. It was probably his intention—if so desultory and irresponsible an individual could be said to have an intention—to make an attempt upon the Island of Walcheren. If such important cities as Flushing and Middelburg could be gained, he thought it possible to prevent the armed invasion now soon expected from Spain. Orange had sent an officer to those cities, who was to reconnoitre their condition, and to advise them against receiving a garrison from government without his authority. So far he connived at Brederode's proceedings, as he had a perfect right to do, for Walcheren was within what had been the Prince's government, and he had no disposition that these cities should share the fate of Tourney, Valenciennes, Bois le Duc, and other towns which had already passed or were passing under the spears of foreign mercenaries.

It is also probable that he did not take any special pains to check the enrolments of Brederode. The peace of Antwerp was not endangered, and to the preservation of that city the Prince seemed now to limit himself. He was hereditary burgrave of Antwerp, but officer of Philip's never more. Despite the shrill demands of Duchess Margaret, therefore; the Prince did not take very active measures by which the crown of Philip might be secured. He, perhaps, looked upon the struggle almost with indifference. Nevertheless, he issued a formal proclamation by which the Count's enlistments were forbidden. Van der Aa, a gentleman who had been active in making these levies, was compelled to leave the city. Brederode was already gone to the north to busy himself with further enrolments.

In the mean time there had been much alarm in Brussels. Egmont, who omitted no opportunity of manifesting his loyalty, offered to throw himself at once into the Isle of Walcheren, for the purpose of dislodging any rebels who might have effected an entrance. He collected accordingly seven or eight hundred Walloon veterans, at his disposal in Flanders, in the little port of Sas de Ghent, prepared at once to execute his intention, "worthy," says a Catholic writer, "of his well-known courage and magnanimity." The Duchess expressed gratitude for the Count's devotion and loyalty, but his services in the sequel proved unnecessary. The rebels, several boat-loads of whom had been cruising about in the neighborhood of Flushing during the early part of March, had been refused admittance into any of the ports on the island. They therefore sailed up the Scheld, and landed at a little village called Ostrawell, at the distance of somewhat more than a mile from Antwerp.

The commander of the expedition was Marnix of Tholouse, brother to Marnix of Saint Aldegonde. This young nobleman, who had left college to fight for the cause of religious liberty, was possessed of fine talents and accomplishments. Like his illustrious brother, he was already a sincere convert to the doctrines of the reformed Church. He had nothing, however, but courage to recommend him as a leader in a military expedition. He was a mere boy, utterly without experience in the field. His troops were raw levies, vagabonds and outlaws.

Such as it was, however, his army was soon posted at Ostrawell in a convenient position, and with considerable judgment. He had the Scheld and its dykes in his rear, on his right and left the dykes and the village. In front he threw up a breastwork and sunk a trench. Here then was set up the standard of rebellion, and hither flocked daily many malcontents from the country round. Within a few days three thousand men were in his camp. On the other handy Brederode was busy in Holland, and boasted of taking the field ere long with six thousand soldiers at the very least. Together they would march to the relief of Valenciennes, and dictate peace in Brussels.

It was obvious that this matter could not be allowed to go on. The Duchess, with some trepidation, accepted the offer made by Philip de Lannoy, Seigneur de Beauvoir, commander of her body-guard in Brussels, to destroy this nest of rebels without delay. Half the whole number of these soldiers was placed at his disposition, and Egmont supplied De Beauvoir with four hundred of his veteran Walloons.

With a force numbering only eight hundred, but all picked men, the intrepid officer undertook his enterprise, with great despatch and secrecy. Upon the 12th March, the whole troop was sent off in small parties, to avoid suspicion, and armed only with sword and dagger. Their helmets, bucklers, arquebusses, corselets, spears, standards and drums, were delivered to their officers, by whom they were conveyed noiselessly to the place of rendezvous. Before daybreak, upon the following morning, De Beauvoir met his soldiers at the abbey of Saint Bernard, within a league of Antwerp. Here he gave them their arms, supplied them with refreshments, and made them a brief speech. He instructed them that they were to advance, with furled banners and without beat of drum, till within sight of the enemy, that the foremost section was to deliver its fire, retreat to the rear and load, to be followed by the next, which was to do the same, and above all, that not an arquebus should be discharged till the faces of the enemy could be distinguished.

The troop started. After a few minutes' march they were in full sight of Ostrawell. They then displayed their flags and advanced upon the fort with loud huzzas. Tholouse was as much taken by surprise as if they had suddenly emerged from the bowels of the earth. He had been informed that the government at Brussels was in extreme trepidation. When he first heard the advancing trumpets and sudden shouts, he thought it a detachment of Brederode's promised force. The cross on the banners soon undeceived him. Nevertheless "like a brave and generous young gentleman as he was," he lost no time in drawing up his men for action, implored them to defend their breastworks, which were impregnable against so small a force, and instructed them to wait patiently with their fire, till the enemy were near enough to be marked.

These orders were disobeyed. The "young scholar," as De Beauvoir had designated him, had no power to infuse his own spirit into his rabble rout of followers. They were already panic-struck by the unexpected appearance of the enemy. The Catholics came on with the coolness of veterans, taking as deliberate aim as if it had been they, not their enemies, who were behind breastworks. The troops of Tholouse fired wildly, precipitately, quite over the heads of the assailants. Many of the defenders were slain as fast as they showed themselves above their bulwarks. The ditch was crossed, the breastwork carried at, a single determined charge. The rebels made little resistance, but fled as soon as the enemy entered their fort. It was a hunt, not a battle. Hundreds were stretched dead in the camp; hundreds were driven into the Scheld; six or eight hundred took refuge in a farm-house; but De Beauvoir's men set fire to the building, and every rebel who had entered it was burned alive or shot. No quarter was given. Hardly a man of the three thousand who had held the fort escaped. The body of Tholouse was cut into a hundred pieces. The Seigneur de Beauvoir had reason, in the brief letter which gave an account of this exploit, to assure her Highness that there were "some very valiant fellows in his little troop." Certainly they had accomplished the enterprise entrusted to them with promptness, neatness, and entire success. Of the great rebellious gathering, which every day had seemed to grow more formidable, not a vestige was left.

This bloody drama had been enacted in full sight of Antwerp. The fight had lasted from daybreak till ten o'clock in the forenoon, during the whole of which period, the city ramparts looking towards Ostrawell, the roofs of houses, the towers of churches had been swarming with eager spectators. The sound of drum and trumpet, the rattle of musketry, the shouts of victory, the despairing cries of the vanquished were heard by thousands who deeply sympathized with the rebels thus enduring so sanguinary a chastisement. In Antwerp there were forty thousand people opposed to the Church of Rome. Of this number the greater proportion were Calvinists, and of these Calvinists there were thousands looking down from the battlements upon the disastrous fight.

The excitement soon became uncontrollable. Before ten o'clock vast numbers of sectaries came pouring towards the Red Gate, which afforded the readiest egress to the scene of action; the drawbridge of the Ostrawell Gate having been destroyed the night before by command of Orange. They came from every street and alley of the city. Some were armed with lance, pike, or arquebus; some bore sledge-hammers; others had the partisans, battle-axes, and huge two-handed swords of the previous century; all were determined upon issuing forth to the rescue of their friends in the fields outside the town. The wife of Tholouse, not yet aware of her husband's death, although his defeat was obvious, flew from street to street, calling upon the Calvinists to save or to avenge their perishing brethren.

A terrible tumult prevailed. Ten thousand men were already up and in arms.—It was then that the Prince of Orange, who was sometimes described by his enemies as timid and pusillanimous by nature, showed the mettle he was made of. His sense of duty no longer bade him defend the crown of Philip—which thenceforth was to be entrusted to the hirelings of the Inquisition—but the vast population of Antwerp, the women, the children, and the enormous wealth of the richest Deity in the world had been confided to his care, and he had accepted the responsibility. Mounting his horse, he made his appearance instantly at the Red Gate, before as formidable a mob as man has ever faced. He came there almost alone, without guards. Hoogstraaten arrived soon afterwards with the same intention. The Prince was received with howls of execration. A thousand hoarse voices called him the Pope's servant, minister of Antichrist, and lavished upon him many more epithets of the same nature. His life was in imminent danger. A furious clothier levelled an arquebus full at his breast. "Die, treacherous villain?" he cried; "thou who art the cause that our brethren have perished thus miserably in yonder field." The loaded weapon was struck away by another hand in the crowd, while the Prince, neither daunted by the ferocious demonstrations against his life, nor enraged by the virulent abuse to which he was subjected, continued tranquilly, earnestly, imperatively to address the crowd. William of Orange had that in his face and tongue "which men willingly call master- authority." With what other talisman could he, without violence and without soldiers, have quelled even for a moment ten thousand furious Calvinists, armed, enraged against his person, and thirsting for vengeance on Catholics. The postern of the Red Gate had already been broken through before Orange and his colleague, Hoogstraaten, had arrived. The most excited of the Calvinists were preparing to rush forth upon the enemy at Ostrawell. The Prince, after he had gained the ear of the multitude, urged that the battle was now over, that the reformers were entirely cut to pieces, the enemy, retiring, and that a disorderly and ill-armed mob would be unable to retrieve the fortunes of the day. Many were persuaded to abandon the design. Five hundred of the most violent, however, insisted upon leaving the gates, and the governors, distinctly warning these zealots that their blood must be upon their own heads, reluctantly permitted that number to issue from the city. The rest of the mob, not appeased, but uncertain, and disposed to take vengeance upon the Catholics within the walls, for the disaster which had been occurring without, thronged tumultuously to the long, wide street, called the Mere, situate in the very heart of the city.

Meantime the ardor of those who had sallied from the gate grew sensibly cooler, when they found themselves in the open fields. De Beauvoir, whose men, after the victory, had scattered in pursuit of the fugitives, now heard the tumult in the city. Suspecting an attack, he rallied his compact little army again for a fresh encounter. The last of the vanquished Tholousians who had been captured; more fortunate than their predecessors, had been spared for ransom. There were three hundred of them; rather a dangerous number of prisoners for a force of eight hundred, who were just going into another battle. De Beauvoir commanded his soldiers, therefore, to shoot them all. This order having been accomplished, the Catholics marched towards Antwerp, drums beating, colors flying. The five hundred Calvinists, not liking their appearance, and being in reality outnumbered, retreated within; the gates as hastily as they had just issued from them. De Beauvoir advanced close to the city moat, on the margin of which he planted the banners of the unfortunate Tholouse, and sounded a trumpet of defiance. Finding that the citizens had apparently no stomach for the fight, he removed his trophies, and took his departure.

On the other hand, the tumult within the walls had again increased. The Calvinists had been collecting in great numbers upon the Mere. This was a large and splendid thoroughfare, rather an oblong market-place than a street, filled with stately buildings, and communicating by various cross streets with the Exchange and with many other public edifices. By an early hour in the afternoon twelve or fifteen thousand Calvinists, all armed and fighting men, had assembled upon the place. They had barricaded the whole precinct with pavements and upturned wagons. They had already broken into the arsenal and obtained many field-pieces, which were planted at the entrance of every street and by-way. They had stormed the city jail and liberated the prisoners, all of whom, grateful and ferocious, came to swell the numbers who defended the stronghold on the Mere. A tremendous mischief was afoot. Threats of pillaging the churches and the houses of the Catholics, of sacking the whole opulent city, were distinctly heard among this powerful mob, excited by religious enthusiasm, but containing within one great heterogeneous mass the elements of every crime which humanity can commit. The alarm throughout the city was indescribable. The cries of women and children, as they remained in trembling expectation of what the next hour might bring forth, were, said one who heard them, "enough to soften the hardest hearts."

Nevertheless the diligence and courage of the Prince kept pace with the insurrection. He had caused the eight companies of guards enrolled in September, to be mustered upon the square in front of the city hall, for the protection of that building and of the magistracy. He had summoned the senate of the city, the board of ancients, the deans of guilds, the ward masters, to consult with him at the council-room. At the peril of his life he had again gone before the angry mob in the Mere, advancing against their cannon and their outcries, and compelling them to appoint eight deputies to treat with him and the magistrates at the town-hall. This done, quickly but deliberately he had drawn up six articles, to which those deputies gave their assent, and in which the city government cordially united. These articles provided that the keys of the city should remain in the possession of the Prince and of Hoogstraaten, that the watch should be held by burghers and soldiers together, that the magistrates should permit the entrance of no garrison, and that the citizens should be entrusted with the care of, the charters, especially with that of the joyful entrance.

These arrangements, when laid before the assembly at the Mere by their deputies, were not received with favor. The Calvinists demanded the keys of the city. They did not choose to be locked up at the mercy of any man. They had already threatened to blow the city hall into the air if the keys were not delivered to them. They claimed that burghers, without distinction of religion, instead of mercenary troops, should be allowed to guard the market-place in front of the town-hall.

It was now nightfall, and no definite arrangement had been concluded. Nevertheless, a temporary truce was made, by means of a concession as to the guard. It was agreed that the burghers, Calvinists and Lutherans, as well as Catholics, should be employed to protect the city. By subtlety, however, the Calvinists detailed for that service, were posted not in the town-house square, but on the ramparts and at the gates.

A night of dreadful expectation was passed. The army of fifteen thousand mutineers remained encamped and barricaded on the Mere, with guns loaded and artillery pointed. Fierce cries of "Long live the beggars,"—"Down with the papists," and other significant watchwords, were heard all night long, but no more serious outbreak occurred.

During the whole of the following day, the Calvinists remained in their encampment, the Catholics and the city guardsmen at their posts near the city hall. The Prince was occupied in the council-chamber from morning till night with the municipal authorities, the deputies of "the religion," and the guild officers, in framing a new treaty of peace. Towards evening fifteen articles were agreed upon, which were to be proposed forthwith to the insurgents, and in case of nonacceptance to be enforced. The arrangement provided that there should be no garrison; that the September contracts permitting the reformed worship at certain places within the city should be maintained; that men of different parties should refrain from mutual insults; that the two governors, the Prince and Hoogstraaten, should keep the keys; that the city should be guarded by both soldiers and citizens, without distinction of religious creed; that a band of four hundred cavalry and a small flotilla of vessels of war should be maintained for the defence of the place, and that the expenses to be incurred should be levied upon all classes, clerical and lay, Catholic and Reformed, without any exception.

It had been intended that the governors, accompanied by the magistrates, should forthwith proceed to the Mere, for the purpose of laying these terms before the insurgents. Night had, however, already arrived, and it was understood that the ill-temper of the Calvinists had rather increased than diminished, so that it was doubtful whether the arrangement would be accepted. It was, therefore, necessary to await the issue of another day, rather than to provoke a night battle in the streets.

During the night the Prince labored incessantly to provide against the dangers of the morrow. The Calvinists had fiercely expressed their disinclination to any reasonable arrangement. They had threatened, without farther pause, to plunder the religious houses and the mansions of all the wealthy Catholics, and to drive every papist out of town. They had summoned the Lutherans to join with them in their revolt, and menaced them, in case of refusal, with the same fate which awaited the Catholics. The Prince, who was himself a Lutheran, not entirely free from the universal prejudice against the Calvinists, whose sect he afterwards embraced, was fully aware of the deplorable fact, that the enmity at that day between Calvinists and Lutherans was as fierce as that between Reformers and Catholics. He now made use of this feeling, and of his influence with those of the Augsburg Confession, to save the city. During the night he had interviews with the ministers and notable members of the Lutheran churches, and induced them to form an alliance upon this occasion with the Catholics and with all friends of order, against an army of outlaws who were threatening to burn and sack the city. The Lutherans, in the silence of night, took arms and encamped, to the number of three or four thousand, upon the river side, in the neighborhood of Saint Michael's cloister. The Prince also sent for the deans of all the foreign mercantile associations—Italian, Spanish, Portuguese, English, Hanseatic, engaged their assistance also for the protection of the city, and commanded them to remain in their armor at their respective factories, ready to act at a moment's warning. It was agreed that they should be informed at frequent intervals as to the progress of events.

On the morning of the 15th, the city of Antwerp presented a fearful sight. Three distinct armies were arrayed at different points within its walls. The Calvinists, fifteen thousand strong, lay in their encampment on the Mere; the Lutherans, armed, and eager for action, were at St. Michael's; the Catholics and the regulars of the city guard were posted on the square. Between thirty-five and forty thousand men were up, according to the most moderate computation. All parties were excited, and eager for the fray. The fires of religious hatred burned fiercely in every breast. Many malefactors and outlaws, who had found refuge in the course of recent events at Antwerp, were in the ranks of the Calvinists, profaning a sacred cause, and inspiring a fanatical party with bloody resolutions. Papists, once and forever, were to be hunted down, even as they had been for years pursuing Reformers. Let the men who had fed fat on the spoils of plundered Christians be dealt with in like fashion. Let their homes be sacked, their bodies given to the dogs—such were the cries uttered by thousands of armed men.

On the other hand, the Lutherans, as angry and as rich as the Catholics, saw in every Calvinist a murderer and a robber. They thirsted after their blood; for the spirit of religious frenzy; the characteristic of the century, can with difficulty be comprehended in our colder and more sceptical age. There was every probability that a bloody battle was to be fought that day in the streets of Antwerp—a general engagement, in the course of which, whoever might be the victors, the city was sure to be delivered over to fire, sack, and outrage. Such would have been the result, according to the concurrent testimony of eye-witnesses, and contemporary historians of every country and creed, but for the courage and wisdom of one man. William of Orange knew what would be the consequence of a battle, pent up within the walls of Antwerp. He foresaw the horrible havoc which was to be expected, the desolation which would be brought to every hearth in the city. "Never were men so desperate and so willing to fight," said Sir Thomas Gresham, who had been expecting every hour his summons to share in the conflict. If the Prince were unable that morning to avert the impending calamity, no other power, under heaven, could save Antwerp from destruction.

The articles prepared on the 14th had been already approved by those who represented the Catholic and Lutheran interests. They were read early in the morning to the troops assembled on the square and at St. Michael's, and received with hearty cheers. It was now necessary that the Calvinists should accept them, or that the quarrel should be fought out at once. At ten o'clock, William of Orange, attended by his colleague, Hoogstraaten, together with a committee of the municipal authorities, and followed by a hundred troopers, rode to the Mere. They wore red scarfs over their armor, as symbols by which all those who had united to put down the insurrection were distinguished. The fifteen thousand Calvinists, fierce and disorderly as ever, maintained a threatening aspect. Nevertheless, the Prince was allowed to ride into the midst of the square. The articles were then read aloud by his command, after which, with great composure, he made a few observations. He pointed out that the arrangement offered them was founded upon the September concessions, that the right of worship was conceded, that the foreign garrison was forbidden, and that nothing further could be justly demanded or honorably admitted. He told them that a struggle upon their part would be hopeless, for the Catholics and Lutherans, who were all agreed as to the justice of the treaty, outnumbered them by nearly two to one. He, therefore, most earnestly and affectionately adjured them to testify their acceptance to the peace offered by repeating the words with which he should conclude. Then, with a firm voice; the Prince exclaimed, "God Save the King!" It was the last time that those words were ever heard from the lips of the man already proscribed by Philip. The crowd of Calvinists hesitated an instant, and then, unable to resist the tranquil influence, convinced by his reasonable language, they raised one tremendous shout of "Vive le Roi!"

The deed was done, the peace accepted, the dreadful battle averted, Antwerp saved. The deputies of the Calvinists now formally accepted and signed the articles. Kind words were exchanged among the various classes of fellow-citizens, who but an hour before had been thirsting for each other's blood, the artillery and other weapons of war were restored to the arsenals, Calvinists, Lutherans, and Catholics, all laid down their arms, and the city, by three o'clock, was entirely quiet. Fifty thousand armed men had been up, according to some estimates, yet, after three days of dreadful expectation, not a single person had been injured, and the tumult was now appeased.

The Prince had, in truth, used the mutual animosity of Protestant sects to a good purpose; averting bloodshed by the very weapons with which the battle was to have been waged. Had it been possible for a man like William the Silent to occupy the throne where Philip the Prudent sat, how different might have been the history of Spain and the fate of the Netherlands. Gresham was right, however, in his conjecture that the Regent and court would not "take the business well." Margaret of Parma was incapable of comprehending such a mind as that of Orange, or of appreciating its efforts. She was surrounded by unscrupulous and mercenary soldiers, who hailed the coming civil war as the most profitable of speculations. "Factotum" Mansfeld; the Counts Aremberg and Meghem, the Duke of Aerschot, the Sanguinary Noircarmes, were already counting their share in the coming confiscations. In the internecine conflict approaching, there would be gold for the gathering, even if no honorable laurels would wreath their swords. "Meghen with his regiment is desolating the country," wrote William of Orange to the Landgrave of Hesse, "and reducing many people to poverty. Aremberg is doing the same in Friesland. They are only thinking how, under the pretext of religion, they may grind the poor Christians, and grow rich and powerful upon their estates and their blood."

The Seignior de Beauvoir wrote to the Duchess, claiming all the estates of Tholouse, and of his brother St. Aldegonde, as his reward for the Ostrawell victory, while Noircarmes was at this very moment to commence at Valenciennes that career of murder and spoliation which, continued at Mons a few years afterwards, was to load his name with infamy.

From such a Regent, surrounded by such councillors, was the work of William de Nassau's hands to gain applause? What was it to them that carnage and plunder had been spared in one of the richest and most populous cities in Christendom? Were not carnage and plunder the very elements in which they disported themselves? And what more dreadful offence against God and Philip could be committed than to permit, as the Prince had just permitted, the right of worship in a Christian land to Calvinists and Lutherans? As a matter of course, therefore, Margaret of Parma denounced the terms by which Antwerp had been saved as a "novel and exorbitant capitulation," and had no intention of signifying her approbation either to prince or magistrate.

1567 [CHAPTER X]

Valenciennes, whose fate depended so closely upon the issue of these various events, was now trembling to her fall. Noircarmes had been drawing the lines more and more closely about the city, and by a refinement of cruelty had compelled many Calvinists from Tournay to act as pioneers in the trenches against their own brethren in Valenciennes. After the defeat of Tholouse, and the consequent frustration of all Brederode's arrangements to relieve the siege, the Duchess had sent a fresh summons to Valenciennes, together with letters acquainting the citizens with the results of the Ostrawell battle. The intelligence was not believed. Egmont and Aerschot, however, to whom Margaret had entrusted this last mission to the beleaguered town, roundly rebuked the deputies who came to treat with them, for their insolence in daring to doubt the word of the Regent. The two seigniors had established themselves in the Chateau of Beusnage, at a league's distance from Valenciennes. Here they received commissioners from the city, half of whom were Catholics appointed by the magistrates, half Calvinists deputed by the consistories. These envoys were informed that the Duchess would pardon the city for its past offences, provided the gates should now be opened, the garrison received, and a complete suppression of all religion except that of Rome acquiesced in without a murmur. As nearly the whole population was of the Calvinist faith, these terms could hardly be thought favorable. It was, however, added, that fourteen days should be allowed to the Reformers for the purpose of converting their property, and retiring from the country.

The deputies, after conferring with their constituents in the, city, returned on the following day with counter-propositions, which were not more likely to find favor with the government. They offered to accept the garrison, provided the soldiers should live at their own expense, without any tax to the citizens for their board, lodging, or pay. They claimed that all property which had been seized should be restored, all persons accused of treason liberated. They demanded the unconditional revocation of the edict by which the city had been declared rebellious, together with a guarantee from the Knights of the Fleece and the state council that the terms of the propose& treaty should be strictly observed.

As soon as these terms had been read to the two seigniors, the Duke of Aerschot burst into an immoderate fit of laughter. He protested that nothing could be more ludicrous than such propositions, worthy of a conqueror dictating a peace, thus offered by a city closely beleaguered, and entirely at the mercy of the enemy. The Duke's hilarity was not shared by Egmont, who, on the contrary, fell into a furious passion. He swore that the city should be burned about their ears, and that every one of the inhabitants should be put to the sword for the insolent language which they had thus dared to address to a most clement sovereign. He ordered the trembling deputies instantly to return with this peremptory rejection of their terms, and with his command that the proposals of government should be accepted within three days' delay.

The commissioners fell upon their knees at Egmont's feet, and begged for mercy. They implored him at least to send this imperious message by some other hand than theirs, and to permit them to absent themselves from the city. They should be torn limb from limb, they said, by the enraged inhabitants, if they dared to present themselves with such instructions before them. Egmont, however, assured them that they should be sent into the city, bound hand and foot, if they did not instantly obey his orders. The deputies, therefore, with heavy hearts, were fain to return home with this bitter result to their negotiations. The, terms were rejected, as a matter of course, but the gloomy forebodings of the commissioners, as to their own fate at the hands of their fellow-citizens, were not fulfilled.

Instant measures were now taken to cannonade the city. Egmont, at the hazard of his life, descended into the foss, to reconnoitre the works, and to form an opinion as to the most eligible quarter at which to direct the batteries. Having communicated the result of his investigations to Noircarmes, he returned to report all these proceedings to the Regent at Brussels. Certainly the Count had now separated himself far enough from William of Orange, and was manifesting an energy in the cause of tyranny which was sufficiently unscrupulous. Many people who had been deceived by his more generous demonstrations in former times, tried to persuade themselves that he was acting a part. Noircarmes, however—and no man was more competent to decide the question distinctly—expressed his entire confidence in Egmont's loyalty. Margaret had responded warmly to his eulogies, had read with approbation secret letters from Egmont to Noircarmes, and had expressed the utmost respect and affection for "the

Count." Egmont had also lost no time in writing to Philip, informing him that he had selected the most eligible spot for battering down the obstinate city of Valenciennes, regretting that he could not have had the eight or ten military companies, now at his disposal, at an earlier day, in which case he should have been able to suppress many tumults, but congratulating his sovereign that the preachers were all fugitive, the reformed religion suppressed, and the people disarmed. He assured the King that he would neglect no effort to prevent any renewal of the tumults, and expressed the hope that his Majesty would be satisfied with his conduct, notwithstanding the calumnies of which the times were full.

Noircarmes meanwhile, had unmasked his batteries, and opened his fire exactly according to Egmont's suggestions.

The artillery played first upon what was called the "White Tower," which happened to bear this ancient, rhyming inscription:

"When every man receives his own,
And justice reigns for strong and weak,
Perfect shall be this tower of stone,
And all the dumb will learn to speak."

"Quand chacun sera satisfaict,
Et la justice regnera,
Ce boulevard sera parfaict,
Et—la muette parlera."—Valenciennes MS.

For some unknown reason, the rather insipid quatrain was tortured into a baleful prophecy. It was considered very ominous that the battery should be first opened against this Sibylline tower. The chimes, too, which had been playing, all through the siege, the music of Marot's sacred songs, happened that morning to be sounding forth from every belfry the twenty-second psalm: "My God, my God, why hast thou forsaken me?"

It was Palm Sunday, 23d of March. The women and children were going mournfully about the streets, bearing green branches in their hands, and praying upon their knees, in every part of the city. Despair and superstition had taken possession of citizens, who up to that period had justified La Noue's assertion, that none could endure a siege like Huguenots. As soon as the cannonading began, the spirit of the inhabitants seemed to depart. The ministers exhorted their flocks in vain as the tiles and chimneys began to topple into the streets, and the concussions of the artillery were responded to by the universal wailing of affrighted women.

Upon the very first day after the unmasking of the batteries, the city sent to Noircarmes, offering almost an unconditional surrender. Not the slightest breach had been effected—not the least danger of an assault existed—yet the citizens, who had earned the respect of their antagonists by the courageous manner in which they had sallied and skirmished during the siege, now in despair at any hope of eventual succor, and completely demoralized by the course of recent events outside their walls, surrendered ignominiously, and at discretion. The only stipulation agreed to by Noircarmes was, that the city should not be sacked, and that the lives of the inhabitants should be spared.

This pledge was, however, only made to be broken. Noircarmes entered the city and closed the gates. All the richest citizens, who of course were deemed the most criminal, were instantly arrested. The soldiers, although not permitted formally to sack the city, were quartered upon the inhabitants, whom they robbed and murdered, according to the testimony of a Catholic citizen, almost at their pleasure.

Michael Herlin, a very wealthy and distinguished burgher, was arrested upon the first day. The two ministers, Guido de Bray and Peregrine de la Grange, together with the son of Herlin, effected their escape by the water-gate. Having taken refuge in a tavern at Saint Arnaud, they were observed, as they sat at supper, by a peasant, who forthwith ran off to the mayor of the borough with the intelligence that some individuals, who looked like fugitives, had arrived at Saint Arnaud. One of them, said the informer, was richly dressed; and wore a gold-hilted sword with velvet scabbard. By the description, the mayor recognized Herlin the younger,—and suspected his companions. They were all arrested, and sent to Noircarmes. The two Herlins, father and son, were immediately beheaded. Guido de Bray and Peregrine de la Grange were loaded with chains, and thrown into a filthy dungeon, previously to their being hanged. Here they were visited by the Countess de Roeulx, who was curious to see how the Calvinists sustained themselves in their martyrdom. She asked them how they could sleep, eat, or drink, when covered with such heavy fetters. "The cause, and my good conscience," answered De Bray, "make me eat, drink, and sleep better than those who are doing me wrong. These shackles are more honorable to me than golden rings and chains. They are more useful to me, and as I hear their clank, methinks I hear the music of sweet voices and the tinkling of lutes."

This exultation never deserted these courageous enthusiasts. They received their condemnation to death "as if it had been an invitation to a marriage feast." They encouraged the friends who crowded their path to the scaffold with exhortations to remain true in the Reformed faith. La Grange, standing upon the ladder, proclaimed with a loud voice, that he was slain for having preached the pure word of God to a Christian people in a Christian land. De Bray, under the same gibbet; testified stoutly that he, too, had committed that offence alone. He warned his friends to obey the magistrates, and all others in authority, except in matters of conscience; to abstain from sedition; but to obey the will of God. The executioner threw him from the ladder while he was yet speaking. So ended the lives of two eloquent, learned, and highly-gifted divines.

Many hundreds of victims were sacrificed in the unfortunate city. "There were a great many other citizens strangled or beheaded," says an aristocratic Catholic historian of the time, "but they were mostly personages of little quality, whose names are quite unknown to me."— [Pontus Payen]—The franchises of the city were all revoked. There was a prodigious amount of property confiscated to the benefit of Noircarmes and the rest of the "Seven Sleepers." Many Calvinists were burned, others were hanged. "For—two whole years," says another Catholic, who was a citizen of Valenciennes at the time, "there was, scarcely a week in which several citizens were not executed and often a great number were despatched at a time. All this gave so much alarm to the good and innocent, that many quitted the city as fast as they could." If the good and innocent happened to be rich, they might be sure that Noircarmes would deem that a crime for which no goodness and innocence could atone.

Upon the fate of Valenciennes had depended, as if by common agreement, the whole destiny of the anti-Catholic party. "People had learned at last," says another Walloon, "that the King had long arms, and that he had not been enlisting soldiers to string beads. So they drew in their horns and their evil tempers, meaning to put them forth again, should the government not succeed at the siege of Valenciennes." The government had succeeded, however, and the consternation was extreme, the general submission immediate and even abject. "The capture of Valenciennes," wrote Noircarmes to Granvelle, "has worked a miracle. The other cities all come forth to meet me, putting the rope around their own necks." No opposition was offered any where. Tournay had been crushed; Valenciennes, Bois le Duc, and all other important places, accepted their garrisons without a murmur. Even Antwerp had made its last struggle, and as soon as the back of Orange was turned, knelt down in the dust to receive its bridle. The Prince had been able, by his courage and wisdom, to avert a sanguinary conflict within its walls, but his personal presence alone could guarantee any thing like religious liberty for the inhabitants, now that the rest of the country was subdued. On the 26th April, sixteen companies of infantry, under Count Mansfeld, entered the gates. On the 28th the Duchess made a visit to the city, where she was received with respect, but where her eyes were shocked by that which she termed the "abominable, sad, and hideous spectacle of the desolated churches."

To the eyes of all who loved their fatherland and their race, the sight of a desolate country, with its ancient charters superseded by brute force, its industrious population swarming from the land in droves, as if the pestilence were raging, with gibbets and scaffolds erected in every village, and with a Sickening and universal apprehension of still darker disasters to follow, was a spectacle still more sad, hideous, and abominable.

For it was now decided that the Duke of Alva, at the head of a Spanish army, should forthwith take his departure for the Netherlands. A land already subjugated was to be crushed, and every vestige of its ancient liberties destroyed. The conquered provinces, once the abode of municipal liberty, of science, art, and literature, and blessed with an unexampled mercantile and manufacturing prosperity, were to be placed in absolute subjection to the cabinet council at Madrid. A dull and malignant bigot, assisted by a few Spanish grandees, and residing at the other extremity of Europe, was thenceforth to exercise despotic authority over countries which for centuries had enjoyed a local administration, and a system nearly approaching to complete self-government. Such was the policy devised by Granvelle and Spinosa, which the Duke of Alva, upon the 15th April, had left Madrid to enforce.

It was very natural that Margaret of Parma should be indignant at being thus superseded. She considered herself as having acquired much credit by the manner in which the latter insurrectionary movements had been suppressed, so soon as Philip, after his endless tergiversations, had supplied her with arms and money. Therefore she wrote in a tone of great asperity to her brother, expressing her discontent. She had always been trammelled in her action, she said, by his restrictions upon her authority. She complained that he had no regard for her reputation or her peace of mind. Notwithstanding, all impediments and dangers, she had at last settled the country, and now another person was to reap the honor. She also despatched the Seigneur de Billy to Spain, for the purpose of making verbal representations to his Majesty upon the inexpediency of sending the Duke of Alva to the Netherlands at that juncture with a Spanish army.

Margaret gained nothing, however, by her letters and her envoy, save a round rebuke from Philip, who was not accustomed to brook the language of remonstrance; even from his sister. His purpose was fixed. Absolute submission was now to be rendered by all. "He was highly astonished and dissatisfied," he said, "that she should dare to write to him with so much passion, and in so resolute a manner. If she received no other recompense, save the glory of having restored the service of God, she ought to express her gratitude to the King for having given her the opportunity of so doing."

The affectation of clement intentions was still maintained, together with the empty pretence of the royal visit. Alva and his army were coming merely to prepare the way for the King, who still represented himself as "debonair and gentle, slow to anger, and averse from bloodshed." Superficial people believed that the King was really coming, and hoped wonders from his advent. The Duchess knew better. The Pope never believed in it, Granvelle never believed in it, the Prince of Orange never believed in it, Councillor d'Assonleville never believed in it. "His Majesty," says the Walloon historian, who wrote from Assonleville's papers, "had many imperative reasons for not coming. He was fond of quiet, he was a great negotiator, distinguished for phlegm and modesty, disinclined to long journeys, particularly to sea voyages, which were very painful to him. Moreover, he was then building his Escorial with so much taste and affection that it was impossible for him to leave home." These excellent reasons sufficed to detain the monarch, in whose place a general was appointed, who, it must be confessed, was neither phlegmatic nor modest, and whose energies were quite equal to the work required. There had in truth never been any thing in the King's project of visiting the Netherlands but pretence.

On the other hand, the work of Orange for the time was finished. He had saved Antwerp, he had done his best to maintain the liberties of the country, the rights of conscience, and the royal authority, so far as they were compatible with each other. The alternative had now been distinctly forced upon every man, either to promise blind obedience or to accept the position of a rebel. William of Orange had thus become a rebel. He had been requested to sign the new oath, greedily taken by the Mansfelds, the Berlaymont, the Aerachot, and the Egmonts, to obey every order which he might receive, against every person and in every place, without restriction or limitation,—and he had distinctly and repeatedly declined the demand. He had again and again insisted upon resigning all his offices. The Duchess, more and more anxious to gain over such an influential personage to the cause of tyranny, had been most importunate in her requisitions. "A man with so noble a heart," she wrote to the Prince, "and with a descent from, such illustrious and loyal ancestors, can surely not forget his duties to his Majesty and the country."

William of Orange knew his duty to both better than the Duchess could understand. He answered this fresh summons by reminding her that he had uniformly refused the new and extraordinary pledge required of him. He had been true to his old oaths, and therefore no fresh pledge was necessary. Moreover, a pledge without limitation he would never take. The case might happen, he said, that he should be ordered to do things contrary to his conscience, prejudicial to his Majesty's service, and in violation of his oaths to maintain the laws of the country. He therefore once more resigned all his offices, and signified his intention of leaving the provinces.

Margaret had previously invited him to an interview at Brussels, which he had declined, because he had discovered a conspiracy in that place to "play him a trick." Assonleville had already been sent to him without effect. He had refused to meet a deputation of Fleece Knights at Mechlin, from the same suspicion of foul play. After the termination of the Antwerp tumult, Orange again wrote to the Duchess, upon the 19th March, repeating his refusal to take the oath, and stating that he considered himself as at least suspended from all his functions, since she had refused, upon the ground of incapacity, to accept his formal resignation. Margaret now determined, by the advice of the state council, to send Secretary Berty, provided with an ample letter of instructions, upon a special mission to the Prince at Antwerp. That respectable functionary performed his task with credit, going through the usual formalities, and adducing the threadbare arguments in favor of the unlimited oath, with much adroitness and decorum. He mildly pointed out the impropriety of laying down such responsible posts as those which the Prince now occupied at such a juncture. He alluded to the distress which the step must occasion to the debonair sovereign.

William of Orange became somewhat impatient under the official lecture of this secretary to the privy council, a mere man of sealing-wax and protocols. The slender stock of platitudes with which he had come provided was soon exhausted. His arguments shrivelled at once in the scorn with which the Prince received them. The great statesman, who, it was hoped, would be entrapped to ruin, dishonor, and death by such very feeble artifices, asked indignantly whether it were really expected that he should acknowledge himself perjured to his old obligations by now signing new ones; that he should disgrace himself by an unlimited pledge which might require him to break his oaths to the provincial statutes and to the

Emperor; that he should consent to administer the religious edicts which he abhorred; that he should act as executioner of Christians on account of their religious opinions, an office against which his soul revolted; that he should bind himself by an unlimited promise which might require, him to put his own wife to death, because she was a Lutheran? Moreover, was it to be supposed that he would obey without restriction any orders issued to him in his Majesty's name, when the King's representative might be a person whose supremacy it ill became one of his' race to acknowledge? Was William of Orange to receive absolute commands from the Duke of Alva? Having mentioned that name with indignation, the Prince became silent.

It was very obvious that no impression was to be made upon the man by formalists. Poor Berty having conjugated his paradigm conscientiously through all its moods and tenses, returned to his green board in the council-room with his proces verbal of the conference. Before he took his leave, however, he prevailed upon Orange to hold an interview with the Duke of Aerschot, Count Mansfeld, and Count Egmont.

This memorable meeting took place at Willebroek, a village midway between Antwerp and Brussels, in the first week of April. The Duke of Aerschot was prevented from attending, but Mansfeld and Egmont—accompanied by the faithful Berty, to make another proces verbal—duly made their appearance. The Prince had never felt much sympathy with Mansfeld, but a tender and honest friendship had always existed between himself and Egmont, notwithstanding the difference of their characters, the incessant artifices employed by the Spanish court to separate them, and the impassable chasm which now, existed between their respective positions towards the government.

The same common-places of argument and rhetoric were now discussed between Orange and the other three personages, the, Prince distinctly stating, in conclusion, that he considered himself as discharged from all his offices, and that he was about to leave the Netherlands for Germany. The interview, had it been confined to such formal conversation, would have but little historic interest. Egmont's choice had been made. Several months before he had signified his determination to hold those for enemies who should cease to conduct themselves as faithful vassals, declared himself to be without fear that the country was to be placed in the hands of Spaniards, and disavowed all intention, in any case whatever, of taking arms against the King. His subsequent course, as we have seen, had been entirely in conformity with these solemn declarations. Nevertheless, the Prince, to whom they had been made, thought it still possible to withdraw his friend from the precipice upon which he stood, and to save him from his impending fate. His love for Egmont had, in his own noble; and pathetic language, "struck its roots too deeply into his heart" to permit him, in this their parting interview, to neglect a last effort, even if this solemn warning were destined to be disregarded.

By any reasonable construction of history, Philip was an unscrupulous usurper, who was attempting to convert himself from a Duke of Brabant and a Count of Holland into an absolute king. It was William who was maintaining, Philip who was destroying; and the monarch who was thus blasting the happiness of the provinces, and about to decimate their population, was by the same process to undermine his own power forever, and to divest himself of his richest inheritance. The man on whom he might have leaned for support, had he been capable of comprehending his character, and of understanding the age in which he had himself been called upon to reign, was, through Philip's own insanity, converted into the instrument by which his most valuable provinces were, to be taken from him, and eventually re-organized into: an independent commonwealth. Could a vision, like that imagined by the immortal dramatist for another tyrant and murderer, have revealed the future to Philip, he, too, might have beheld his victim, not crowned himself, but pointing to a line of kings, even to some who 'two-fold balls and treble sceptres carried', and smiling on them for his. But such considerations as these had no effect upon the Prince of Orange. He knew himself already proscribed, and he knew that the secret condemnation had extended to Egmont also. He was anxious that his friend should prefer the privations of exile, with the chance of becoming the champion of a struggling country, to the wretched fate towards which his blind confidence was leading him. Even then it seemed possible that the brave soldier, who had been recently defiling his sword in the cause of tyranny, might be come mindful of his brighter and earlier fame. Had Egmont been as true to his native land as, until "the long divorce of steel fell on him," he was faithful to Philip, he might yet have earned brighter laurels than those gained at St. Quentin and Gravelines. Was he doomed to fall, he might find a glorious death upon freedom's battle-field, in place of that darker departure then so near him, which the prophetic language of Orange depicted, but which he was too sanguine to fear. He spoke with confidence of the royal clemency. "Alas, Egmont," answered the Prince, "the King's clemency, of which you boast, will destroy you. Would that I might be deceived, but I foresee too clearly that you are to be the bridge which the Spaniards will destroy so soon as they have passed over it to invade our country." With these last, solemn words he concluded his appeal to awaken the Count from his fatal security. Then, as if persuaded that he was looking upon his friend for the last time, William of Orange threw his arms around Egmont, and held him for a moment in a close embrace. Tears fell from the eyes of both at this parting moment—and then the brief scene of simple and lofty pathos terminated—Egmont and Orange separated from each other, never to meet again on earth.

A few days afterwards, Orange addressed a letter to Philip once more resigning all his offices, and announcing his intention of departing from the Netherlands for Germany. He added, that he should be always ready to place himself and his property at the King's orders in every thing which he believed conducive to the true service of his Majesty. The Prince had already received a remarkable warning from old Landgrave Philip of Hesse, who had not forgotten the insidious manner in which his own memorable captivity had been brought about by the arts of Granvelle and of Alva. "Let them not smear your mouths with honey," said the Landgrave. "If the three seigniors, of whom the Duchess Margaret has had so much to say, are invited to court by Alva, under pretext of friendly consultation, let them be wary, and think twice ere they accept. I know the Duke of Alva and the Spaniards, and how they dealt with me."

The Prince, before he departed, took a final leave of Horn and Egmont, by letters, which, as if aware of the monumental character they were to assume for posterity, he drew up in Latin. He desired, now that he was turning his back upon the country, that those two nobles who had refused to imitate, and had advised against his course, should remember that, he was acting deliberately, conscientiously, and in pursuance of a long- settled plan.

To Count Horn he declared himself unable to connive longer at the sins daily committed against the country and his own conscience. He assured him that the government had been accustoming the country to panniers, in order that it might now accept patiently the saddle and bridle. For himself, he said, his back was not strong enough for the weight already imposed upon it, and he preferred to endure any calamity which might happen to him in exile, rather than be compelled by those whom they had all condemned to acquiesce in the object so long and steadily pursued.

He reminded Egmont, who had been urging him by letter to remain, that his resolution had been deliberately taken, and long since communicated to his friends. He could not, in conscience, take the oath required; nor would he, now that all eyes were turned upon him, remain in the land, the only recusant. He preferred to encounter all that could happen, rather than attempt to please others by the sacrifice of liberty, of his fatherland, of his own conscience. "I hope, therefore," said he to Egmont in conclusion, "that you, after weighing my reasons, will not disapprove my departure. The rest I leave to God, who will dispose of all as may most conduce to the glory of his name. For yourself, I pray you to believe that you have no more sincere friend than I am. My love for you has struck such deep root into my heart, that it can be lessened by no distance of time or place, and I pray you in return to maintain the same feelings towards me which you have always cherished."

The Prince had left Antwerp upon the 11th April, and had written these letters from Breda, upon the 13th of the same month. Upon the 22d, he took his departure for Dillenburg, the ancestral seat of his family in Germany, by the way of Grave and Cleves.

It was not to be supposed that this parting message would influence Egmont's decision with regard to his own movements, when his determination had not been shaken at his memorable interview with the Prince. The Count's fate was sealed. Had he not been praised by Noircarmes; had he not earned the hypocritical commendations of Duchess Margaret; nay more, had he not just received a most affectionate letter of, thanks and approbation from the King of Spain himself? This letter, one of the most striking monuments of Philip's cold-blooded perfidy, was dated the 26th of March. "I am pleased, my cousin," wrote the monarch to Egmont, "that you have taken the new oath, not that I considered it at all necessary so far as regards yourself, but for the example which you have thus given to others, and which I hope they will all follow. I have received not less pleasure in hearing of the excellent manner in which you are doing your duty, the assistance you are rendering, and the offers which you are making to my sister, for which I thank you, and request you to continue in the same course."

The words were written by the royal hand which had already signed the death-warrant of the man to whom they were addressed. Alva, who came provided with full powers to carry out the great scheme resolved upon, unrestrained by provincial laws or by the statutes of the Golden Fleece, had left Madrid to embark for Carthagena, at the very moment when Egmont was reading the royal letter. "The Spanish honey," to use once more old Landgrave Philip's homely metaphor, had done its work, and the unfortunate victim was already entrapped.

Count Horn remained in gloomy silence in his lair at Weert, awaiting the hunters of men, already on their way. It seemed inconceivable that he, too, who knew himself suspected and disliked, should have thus blinded himself to his position. It will be seen, however, that the same perfidy was to be employed to ensnare him which proved so successful with Egmont.

As for the Prince himself, he did not move too soon. Not long after his arrival in Germany, Vandenesse, the King's private secretary, but Orange's secret agent, wrote him word that he had read letters from the King to Alva in which the Duke was instructed to "arrest the Prince as soon as he could lay hands upon him, and not to let his trial last more than twenty-four hours."

Brederode had remained at Viane, and afterwards at Amsterdam, since the ill-starred expedition of Tholouse, which he had organized, but at which he had not assisted. He had given much annoyance to the magistracy of Amsterdam, and to all respectable persons, Calvinist or Catholic. He made much mischief, but excited no hopes in the minds of reformers. He was ever surrounded by a host of pot companions, swaggering nobles disguised as sailors, bankrupt tradesmen, fugitives and outlaws of every description, excellent people to drink the beggars' health and to bawl the beggars' songs, but quite unfit for any serious enterprise. People of substance were wary of him, for they had no confidence in his capacity, and were afraid of his frequent demands for contributions to the patriotic cause. He spent his time in the pleasure gardens, shooting at the mark with arquebuss or crossbow, drinking with his comrades, and shrieking "Vivent les gueux."

The Regent, determined to dislodge him, had sent Secretary La Torre to him in March, with instructions that if Brederode refused to leave Amsterdam, the magistracy were to call for assistance upon Count Meghem, who had a regiment at Utrecht. This clause made it impossible for La Torre to exhibit his instructions to Brederode. Upon his refusal, that personage, although he knew the secretary as well as he knew his own father, coolly informed him that he knew nothing about him; that he did not consider him as respectable a person as he pretended to be; that he did not believe a word of his having any commission from the Duchess, and that he should therefore take no notice whatever of his demands. La Torre answered meekly, that he was not so presumptuous, nor so destitute of sense as to put himself into comparison with a, gentleman of Count Brederode's quality, but that as he had served as secretary to the privy council for twenty-three years, he had thought that he might be believed upon his word. Hereupon La Tome drew up a formal protest, and Brederode drew up another. La Torre made a proces verbal of their interview, while Brederode stormed like a madman, and abused the Duchess for a capricious and unreasonable tyrant. He ended by imprisoning La Torre for a day or two, and seizing his papers. By a singular coincidence, these events took place on the 13th, 24th, and 15th of March, the very days of the great Antwerp tumult. The manner in which the Prince of Orange had been dealing with forty or fifty thousand armed men, anxious to cut each other's throats, while Brederode was thus occupied in browbeating a pragmatical but decent old secretary, illustrated the difference in calibre of the two men.

This was the Count's last exploit. He remained at Amsterdam some weeks longer, but the events which succeeded changed the Hector into a faithful vassal. Before the 12th of April, he wrote to Egmont, begging his intercession with Margaret of Parma, and offering "carte blanche" as to terms, if he might only be allowed to make his peace with government. It was, however, somewhat late in the day for the "great beggar" to make his submission. No terms were accorded him, but he was allowed by the Duchess to enjoy his revenues provisionally, subject to the King's pleasure. Upon the 25th April, he entertained a select circle of friends at his hotel in Amsterdam, and then embarked at midnight for Embden. A numerous procession of his adherents escorted him to the ship, bearing lighted torches, and singing bacchanalian songs. He died within a year afterwards, of disappointment and hard drinking, at Castle Hardenberg, in Germany, after all his fretting and fury, and notwithstanding his vehement protestations to die a poor soldier at the feet of Louis Nassau.

That "good chevalier and good Christian," as his brother affectionately called him, was in Germany, girding himself for the manly work which Providence had destined him to perform. The life of Brederode, who had engaged in the early struggle, perhaps from the frivolous expectation of hearing himself called Count of Holland, as his ancestors had been, had contributed nothing to the cause of freedom, nor did his death occasion regret. His disorderly band of followers dispersed in every direction upon the departure of their chief. A vessel in which Batenburg, Galaina, and other nobles, with their men-at-arms, were escaping towards a German port, was carried into Harlingen, while those gentlemen, overpowered by sleep and wassail, were unaware of their danger, and delivered over to Count Meghem, by the treachery of their pilot. The soldiers, were immediately hanged. The noblemen were reserved to grace the first great scaffold which Alva was to erect upon the horse-market in Brussels.

The confederacy was entirely broken to pieces. Of the chieftains to whom the people had been accustomed to look for support and encouragement, some had rallied to the government, some were in exile, some were in prison.

Montigny, closely watched in Spain, was virtually a captive, pining for the young bride to whom he had been wedded amid such brilliant festivities but a few months before his departure, and for the child which was never to look upon its father's face.

His colleague, Marquis Berghen, more fortunate, was already dead. The excellent Viglius seized the opportunity to put in a good word for Noircarmes, who had been grinding Tournay in the dust, and butchering the inhabitants of Valenciennes. "We have heard of Berghen's death," wrote the President to his faithful Joachim. "The Lord of Noircarmes, who has been his substitute in the governorship of Hainault, has given a specimen of what he can do. Although I have no private intimacy with that nobleman, I can not help embracing him with all my benevolence. Therefore, oh my Hopper, pray do your best to have him appointed governor."

With the departure of Orange, a total eclipse seemed to come over the Netherlands. The country was absolutely helpless, the popular heart cold with apprehension. All persons at all implicated in the late troubles, or suspected of heresy, fled from their homes. Fugitive soldiers were hunted into rivers, cut to pieces in the fields, hanged, burned, or drowned, like dogs, without quarter, and without remorse. The most industrious and valuable part of the population left the land in droves. The tide swept outwards with such rapidity that the Netherlands seemed fast becoming the desolate waste which they had been before the Christian era. Throughout the country, those Reformers who were unable to effect their escape betook themselves to their old lurking-places. The new religion was banished from all the cities, every conventicle was broken up by armed men, the preachers and leading members were hanged, their disciples beaten with rods, reduced to beggary, or imprisoned, even if they sometimes escaped the scaffold. An incredible number, however, were executed for religious causes. Hardly a village so small, says the Antwerp chronicler,—[Meteren]—but that it could furnish one, two, or three hundred victims to the executioner. The new churches were levelled to the ground, and out of their timbers gallows were constructed. It was thought an ingenious pleasantry to hang the Reformers upon the beams under which they had hoped to worship God. The property of the fugitives was confiscated. The beggars in name became beggars in reality. Many who felt obliged to remain, and who loved their possessions better than their creed, were suddenly converted into the most zealous of Catholics. Persons who had for years not gone to mass, never omitted now their daily and nightly visits to the churches. Persons who had never spoken to an ecclesiastic but with contumely, now could not eat their dinners without one at their table. Many who were suspected of having participated in Calvinistic rites, were foremost and loudest in putting down and denouncing all forms and shows of the reformation. The country was as completely "pacified," to use the conqueror's expression, as Gaul had been by Caesar.

The, Regent issued a fresh edict upon the 24th May, to refresh the memories of those who might have forgotten previous statutes, which were, however, not calculated to make men oblivious. By this new proclamation, all ministers and teachers were sentenced to the gallows. All persons who had suffered their houses to be used for religious purposes were sentenced to the gallows. All parents or masters whose children or servants had attended such meetings were sentenced to the gallows, while the children and servants were only to be beaten with rods. All people who sang hymns at the burial of their relations were sentenced to the gallows. Parents who allowed their newly-born children to be baptized by other hands than those of the Catholic priest were sentenced to the gallows. The same punishment was denounced against the persons who should christen the child or act as its sponsors. Schoolmasters who should teach any error or false doctrine were likewise to be punished with death. Those who infringed the statutes against the buying and selling of religious books and songs were to receive the same doom; after the first offence. All sneers or insults against priests and ecclesiastics were also made capital crimes. Vagabonds, fugitives; apostates, runaway monks, were ordered forthwith to depart from every city on pain of death. In all cases confiscation of the whole property of the criminal was added to the hanging.

This edict, says a contemporary historian, increased the fear of those professing the new religion to such an extent that they left the country "in great heaps." It became necessary, therefore, to issue a subsequent proclamation forbidding all persons, whether foreigners or natives, to leave the land or to send away their property, and prohibiting all shipmasters, wagoners, and other agents of travel, from assisting in the flight of such fugitives, all upon pain of death.

Yet will it be credited that the edict of 24th May, the provisions of which have just been sketched, actually excited the wrath of Philip on account of their clemency? He wrote to the Duchess, expressing the pain and dissatisfaction which he felt, that an edict so indecent, so illegal, so contrary to the Christian religion, should have been published. Nothing, he said, could offend or distress him more deeply, than any outrage whatever, even the slightest one, offered to God and to His Roman Catholic Church.

He therefore commanded his sister instantly to revoke the edict. One might almost imagine from reading the King's letter that Philip was at last appalled at the horrors committed in his name. Alas, he was only indignant that heretics had been suffered to hang who ought to have been burned, and that a few narrow and almost impossible loopholes had been left through which those who had offended alight effect their escape.

And thus, while the country is paralyzed with present and expected woe, the swiftly advancing trumpets of the Spanish army resound from beyond the Alps. The curtain is falling upon the prelude to the great tragedy which the prophetic lips of Orange had foretold. When it is again lifted, scenes of disaster and of bloodshed, battles, sieges, executions, deeds of unfaltering but valiant tyranny, of superhuman and successful resistance, of heroic self-sacrifice, fanatical courage and insane cruelty, both in the cause of the Wrong and the Right, will be revealed in awful succession—a spectacle of human energy, human suffering, and human strength to suffer, such as has not often been displayed upon the stage of the world's events.